THE PRICE OF FREEDOM

We have become free like a bird out of a trap. The net is broken and now we are free.

Psalms 124:7 NLV

By
Franklin N. Abazie

THE PRICE OF FREEDOM

COPYRIGHT@ 2016 BY Franklin N Abazie

ISBN 978-1-94513302-2

All right reserved. This book or any portion thereof may not be reproduced or used in any manner whatsoever without the express written permission of the publisher, except for the use of brief quotations in a book review. All Bible quotes are from King James Version and others as noted. Published by: F N ABAZIE PUBLISHING HOUSE- a.k.a Empowerment Bookstore.

Psalms 26:7 That I may publish with the voice of thanksgiving and tell of all thy wondrous works.

To order additional copies, wholesales or booking: Call the Church office 973-372-7518, or call Empowerment Bookstore Hotline 973-393-8518

Worship address: 343 Sanford Avenue Newark New Jersey 07106

Administrative Head Office address: 33 Schley Street Newark New Jersey 07112 Email:pastorfranknto@yahoo.com

Website www.fnabaziehealingministries.org

Publishing House www.fnabaziepublishinghouse.org

This book is a production of F N Abazie Publishing House. A publication Arms of Miracle of God Ministries 2016
First Edition

CONTENTS

THE MANDATE OF THE COMMISSION............iv

ARMS OF THE COMMISSION................................v

INTRODUCTION..vi

CHAPTER 1

1. The Power of Freedom 24

CHAPTER 2

2. Operating in Freedom..36

CHAPTER 3

3. Experiencing Freedom in Christ...........................49

CHAPTER 4

4. Prayer of Salvation.. 88

CHAPTER 5

5. About the Author..101

THE MANDATE OF THE COMMISSION

"THE MOMENT IS DUE TO IMPACT YOUR WORLD THROUGH THE REVIVAL OF THE HEALING & MIRACLE MINISTRY OF JESUS CHRIST OF NAZARETH.

I AM SENDING YOU TO RESTORE HEALTH UNTO THEE AND I WILL HEAL THEE OF THY WOUNDS, SAID THE LORD OF HOST."

ARMS OF THE COMMISSION

1) F N Abazie Ministries-Miracle of God Ministries (Miracle Chapel Intl)

2) F N Abazie TV Ministries: Global Television Ministry Outreach.

3) F N Abazie Radio Ministries: Radio Broadcasting Outreach.

4) F N Abazie Publishing House: Book Publication.

5) F N Abazie Bible School: also called Word of Healing Bible School (W.O.H.B.S)

6) F N Abazie Evangelistic Ass: Miracle of God Ministries: Global Crusade

7) Empowerment Bookstore: Book distribution.

8) F N Abazie Helping Hands: Meeting the help of the needy world wide

9) F N Abazie Disaster Recovery Mission: Global Disaster Recovery.

10) F N Abazie Prison Ministry: Prison Ministry for all convicts "Second chance"

Some of our ministry arms are waiting the appointed time to commence

INTRODUCTION

"The starting point of all achievement is desire" ---- **Napoleon Hill**

It is my desire to use this publication to shed more light on the reason Jesus Christ died for our sins on the cross. Often times those of the other faith and some sceptic really do need more clarification, It is my joy to write about the price of freedom with strong emphasis on the life, ministry and death of our Master Jesus Christ.

No one else died for our sins but Jesus Christ of Nazareth. We must embrace this truth as evidence of our Salvation.

Salvation means deliverance from sin and redemption of our soul from destruction. So many people misunderstand & misinterpret this scriptural truth. "There is no other way we all can be saved except by the name of Jesus Christ of Nazareth."

"Neither is there salvation in any other: for there is none other name under heaven given among men, whereby we must be saved."
Acts4:12

As believers, we must be armed with the knowledge of the price for our freedom, against the wiles and schemes of the devil. Lest Satan should get an advantage of us: for we are not ignorant of his devices.

"As long as we are not ignorant, of our freedom in Christ, we will forever have the victory against the devil. The power of attorney is in the Name of Jesus Christ. It is inevitable for anyone to be able to purchase their freedom and liberty. He that spared not his own Son, but delivered him up for us all, how shall he not with him also freely give us all things?"
Romans8:32.

Freedom in Christ Jesus grants us access in his divine nature.

"Whereby are given unto us exceeding great and precious promises: that by these ye might be partakers of the divine nature, having escaped the corruption that is in the world through lust."
2peter1:4

For God so loved the world, that he gave his only begotten Son, that whosoever believeth in him should not perish, but have everlasting life.
John3:16

In deed it was out of God's love for man that He sent His only begotten son to save us all from the destruction of the devil. This publication is an expository teaching that reveals some striking truth about the freedom we all enjoy today. In this publication, you will appreciate some relevant teachings on the power of freedom, operating in freedom, experiencing freedom in Christ among the few significant chapters.

Set aside all secular knowledge and come with me as inspired by the Holy Ghost as I pen down this great small yet but impactful manual for the freedom of our spirit, soul, and body from all the wiles and schemes of the devil.

"Christ hath redeemed us from the curse of the law, being made a curse for us: for it is written, Cursed is every one that hangeth on a tree: That the blessing of Abraham might come on the Gentiles through Jesus Christ; that we might receive the promise of the Spirit through faith."

Gal3:13-14

May the Lord richly bless you as you read.

Happy Reading!

Now the Lord is that Spirit:

and where the Spirit of the Lord is, there is liberty.

2Cor3:17

HIS DESTINY WAS THE CROSS....

HIS PURPOSE WAS LOVE.....

HIS REASON WAS YOU....

FREEDOM COUNSEL

"We must first develop the superior mentality of a free person; free from occultism, free from witches and wizards, free from nightmares and satanic harassment. Consider this today and say to yourself, I am a free man. I am a free born. I have the capacity to operate in God's dimension of creation and wisdom. I am fearfully and wonderfully made. No weapon fashioned against me shall ever prosper.

We must develop this understanding that we are seated with Christ far above principalities and power. And hath raised us up together, and made us sit together in heavenly places in Christ Jesus"

Ephesians 2:6

Always chose your friends wisely, for evil companion corrupt good manners.

Remember *"he that walk with the wise shall be wise."*

In the time of prosperity we recognize our friends.

"Wealth maketh many friends."
Proverb19:4

But in the time of adversity our friends know us.

"and there is a friend that sticketh closer than a brother."
Proverb18:24

Always recognize those who make you a special person in their lives. Never make people significant in your life when you are only an option to them. The less you associate with some people the more your life will improve.

Remember Abraham did not become rich until he separated from lot his nephew.

"And the Lord said unto Abram, after that lot was separated from him, Lift up now thine eyes, and look from the place where thou art northward, and southward, and eastward, and westward: For all the land which thou seest, to thee will I give it, and to thy seed for ever."
Genesis13:14-15

Anytime time you allow mediocrity in others, it increases your mediocrity. An important attribute in successful people is their impatience with failure, negative thinking, and mediocrity. As we grow in life, our association will eventually change over time.

Eventually, you will disconnect from those that failed to improve their lives and you will connect and make friends with other successful people going up higher in the race of life.

Never receive counsel from unproductive negative thinking people, never discus your trial and challenges with those incapable of contributing to the solution or solving your problems. Always look for the best in people around you. Develop a forgiving heart, a thankful countenance, and praiseful spirit.

Always remember this, if you are going to achieve excellence in big things, you must develop the habit in little matters.

Collin Powell once said and I quote *"A dream doesn't become a reality through magic, it takes sweat, determination, and hard work."*

There is no secret to success, it is the result of preparation, hard work, and learning from failure." Excellence is not an exception, it is a prevailing attitude.

Among the predominantly threats to freedom is fear of the unknown. Therefore let me give you a few definition of fear.

What is fear?

F......FALSE

E.................EXPERIENCE

A.........................APPEARING

R......................................REAL

F............FACELESS

E..............................ENEMY

A................................AFFLICTING

R..REASONING

F.........FREQUENTLY

E....................EXPECTED

A................................ADVARSITY

R..REALIZED

F............FANTACIZED

E..................EXERGERATION

A..........................ABOVE

R....................................REALITY

F............FIERCE
E....................EMOTION
A............................AROUSING
R...................................RESTLESNESS

F..........FACELESS
E................EXPRESSION
A........................ACKNOWLEDGED
R................................REPEATEDLY

F.........FAILURE
E.................EXPECTED
A............................AND
R.................................REHEARSED

Unless we confront our fears with faith in God, we will never fulfil the will of God concerning our lives. We must operate in faith if we must experience freedom in life.

HOW TO ENFORCE FREEDOM IN CHRIST JESUS

REPENT

The acts of repentance positions us properly to experience genuine Salvation in Jesus Christ. Unless we repent we will forever remain prey and subject to the devil attack and assaults. Repentance as the first step of freedom exonerates and vindicates our spirit soul and body from the condemnation and accusation of the devil.

"There is therefore now no condemnation to them which are in Christ Jesus, who walk not after the flesh, but after the Spirit."
Romans8:1

Repentance here means total surrender to Christ Jesus. God will do nothing for us unless we are willing to surrender our life to him.

WE MUST BE BORN AGAIN

"We must become born again Christian if we must experience a righteous walk with the master Jesus Christ. Until we give our lives to Jesus Christ we are not set for Deliverance and for Salvation. Once we become born again Christians we freely receive the things that are given to us by God. Among which is Salvation which brings total Spiritual freedom. We become children of the Most High God at Salvation. The Spirit itself beareth witness with our spirit, that we are the children of God."
Romans8:16

PRAYER LIFE

For us to sustain our freedom in Christ Jesus, we must have a genuine prayer life. It takes a man/woman of prayer to experience total freedom in all things in life. It is compulsory for all that want to experience total freedom in Christ Jesus to have a prayer life.

PRAYER POINT TO EXPERINCE GENUINE FREEDOM IN CHRIST

1) Heavenly Father grant me open door to experience genuine salvation in the name of Jesus.

2) Hand of God, separate and vindicate me from all curses, spells, and attack of the enemy in the name of Jesus.

3) Spirit of God help my infirmities in the name of Jesus.

4) Father, let the spirit of knowledge, understanding, wisdom, power, might glory overshadow my life in the name of Jesus.

5) Arise Oh God and let all my enemies be scattered.

6) Fire of Elijah arise against agent of darkness assigned against my life.

7) Ancient of day free me from the shackles of the enemy in the name of Jesus.

8) I shall not die but live to declare the works of God in the name of Jesus.

9) I receive protection and deliverance by the power in the name of Jesus.

10) Every agent of the devil assigned to torment destiny, & career die the name of Jesus.

11) Lord God free me from the bondage of sins and immoralities.

12) Spirit of God free and liberate my mind from all condemnation and intimidation in the name of Jesus.

13) Father God destroy every satanic barrier hindering me from progressing in my life in the name of Jesus

14) Power of God, arise and deliver me from every family strong man in the name of Jesus.

15) Every evil altar hindering my prayer be paralyze in the name of Jesus.

16) I decree breakthrough from every chains in Jesus Name.

17) I establish liberty of my soul , spirit and body in the name of Jesus.

18) I decree that all evil men boasting with satanic powers to dominate me die in the name of Jesus.

19) I pled the blood of Jesus over every demonic network in my life.

20) I declare that I must experience liberty in Christ Jesus.

21) Every obstacle that hinders my progress in this land, I command you to be paralyzed and neutralized in the name of Jesus.

22) Any power prolonging my breakthrough, I stop you today in Jesus Name.

23) I destroy every power of the night in the name of Jesus.

24) I paralyze every power of the water working against my life and destiny in the Name of Jesus.

25) Hand of God vindicate me from every false accusation and manipulation in the name of Jesus.

26) Finger of the Lord liberate my spirit from the assault's of the devil.

27) I thank you Jesus for hearing my prayer.

AMEN

CHAPTER 1
THE POWER OF FREEDOM

Now the Lord is that Spirit: and where the Spirit of the Lord is, there is liberty.
2Cor3:17

In search of any kind of freedom there is always a price tag and power attached to it. Jesus died for us to be alive. Jesus paid the ultimate price for the redemption of the life of man.

Contrary to other believes and assertion, Jesus Christ paid the ultimate sacrifice with his blood to purchase for us "power and liberty of life." (Freedom to live our lives freely without any fear or harassment from the devil).

The power of freedom must be understood with our faith in Him.

"He that spared not his own Son, but delivered him up for us all, how shall he not with him also freely give us all things?"
Romans8:32

Chapter 1 - The Power of Freedom

DIFFERENT WAYS TO EXPERIENCE GENUINE FREEDOM IN CHRIST

THROUGH JESUS CHRIST

Jesus Christ brought genuine freedom and liberty for us all. It is written For God so loved the world, that he gave his only begotten Son, that whosoever believeth in him should not perish, but have everlasting life.

"For God sent not his Son into the world to condemn the world; but that the world through him might be saved." **John3:16-17**

If you consider that the wages of sin is death, you will appreciate the death of Jesus Christ on the cross.

"Jesus saith unto him, I am the way, the truth, and the life: no man cometh unto the Father, but by me." **John14:6**.

Unless you encounter the Jesus Christ of Nazareth, you are not a ccandidate for his power. Accept the Lord Jesus and you shall experience the free flow of his redemptive power in freedom and liberty.

THROUGH THE BIBLE

A thorough searching and studying of the bible will grant you a life time encounter with freedom in Christ Jesus. Scripture teaches us that, a person can't be spiritually free unless he has embraced the truth of the word of God.

(Psalms119:130)

"Really, that person must understand how the truth work. And ye shall know the truth, and the truth shall make you free."
John8:32.

"The truth is ageless, it is timeless. The truth is the truth anywhere and anytime of the day. For we can do nothing against the truth, but for the truth."
2cor13:8

Chapter 1 - The Power of Freedom

FREEDOM BY THE HOLY GHOST

It is written *"But there is a spirit in man: and the inspiration of the Almighty giveth them understanding."* **Job32:8**.

It is significant we establish and comprehend freedom by the Holy Spirit. This is the same Spirit that brings liberty.

"But ye shall receive power, after that the Holy Ghost is come upon you, and ye shall be witnesses unto me both in Jerusalem, and in all Judea, and in Samaria, and unto the uttermost part of the earth." **Acts1:8.**

"Freedom by the Holy Spirit means liberty in our lives and career. Now the Lord is that Spirit: and where the Spirit of the Lord is, there is liberty." **2Cor3:17**

FREEDOM BY OBEYING THE LAWS OF GOD

It is the will of God for us all to obey Gods law. God gave us laws and statue as a gateway for us to experience the power of freedom. No one will ever experience God freedom as long as we violates God's law.

Remember... But if ye refuse and rebel, ye shall be devoured with the sword: for the mouth of the Lord hath spoken it.
Isaiah1:20

"Obedience to Gods laws are the gateway to provoke supernatural freedom in Christ Jesus. And I will walk at liberty: for I seek thy precepts."
Psalms119:45

Everybody want to experience freedom in our careers, businesses, marriages e.t.c but most of us are not willing to pay the price for this freedom. God wants us all to obey his commandment.

Chapter 1 - The Power of Freedom

Remember...*For this is the love of God, that we keep his commandments: and his commandments are not grievous.* **1John5:3.**

The power of freedom is engrafted in the blood of Jesus Christ. Until we embrace this teaching we remain powerless in life. Let every soul be subject unto the higher powers."

For there is no power but of God: the powers that be are ordained of God." **Romans13:1.**

"We cannot do the wrong thing and expect the right result. We cannot cheat, lie steal, commit murder and yet expect to experience the power of freedom in Christ Jesus. Great in counsel, and mighty in work: for thine eyes are open upon all the ways of the sons of men: to give every one according to his ways, and according to the fruit of his doings."
Jer32:19.

"Although God is a merciful God, but as long as we disobey his laws and commandment we will never enjoy the benefits of the power of freedom in Christ Jesus. And ye shall know the truth, and the truth shall make you free."
John 8:32

DO YOU REALLY WANT TO EXPERIENCE THE POWER OF FREEDOM?

The power of freedom is free of charge but we must be convinced and convicted to confess Jesus as Lord and our personal savior. God want us to put our life and trust in him. Commit thy way unto the Lord; trust also in him; and he shall bring it to pass.
Psalms 37:5.

"If the Son therefore shall make you free, ye shall be free indeed."
John 8:36

Chapter 1 - The Power of Freedom

WHAT ARE WE SAYING?

"In one sentence, we must experience and know the ways and acts of God for ourselves. He made known his ways unto Moses, his acts unto the children of Israel."
Psalms 103:7.

"We must forsake our sins, repent and confess Jesus Christ as Lord and savior. For anyone to have an encounter with his presence, power to deliver, protect and to enjoy freedom we must develop the consciousness of his presence and the superior mentality that he make intercession for us forever."
2 Corinthians 13:4

For he was crucified in weakness, but lives by the power of God. For we also are weak in him, but in dealing with you we will live with him by the power of God.

Every demonic harassment anyone has ever suffered in life because we lack the mystery of his power. The reason for all the spiritual torture and demonic assaults is because we need an encounter with his real power to save, to deliver and freedom.

"He that committeth sin is of the devil; for the devil sinneth from the beginning. For this purpose the Son of God was manifested, that he might destroy the works of the devil."

1John 3:8

"It is about the greatness of God, not the significance of man. God made man small and the universe big to say something about himself." — **John Piper**

SUMMARY OF CHAPTER ONE

~ It is the power of freedom that grants us boldness and authority.

~ The power of freedom breaks limitation over our lives

~The power of freedom makes encourages us to prevail against any prevailing obstacles.

Chapter 1 - The Power of Freedom

~The power of freedom motivates us to break forth on every side of our lives.

~The power of freedom produces the dignity of our Christianity.

~The power of freedom in Christ Jesus grants us access into the supernatural.

~The power of freedom in Christ Jesus announces us to our world.

~The power of freedom brings healing & health to our body.

DECISION KEYS

1) NOTHING CHANGES UNTIL YOU MAKE UP YOUR MIND

2) DECISION IS THE GATEWAY TO DELIVERANCE.

3) UNTIL YOU DECISDE, NO ONE WILL DECISDE FOR YOU.

4) YOUR PROSPERITY IS PROPORTIONAL TO YOUR DECISIONS.

5) THE DECISION YOU MAKE WILL DETERMINE THE FUTURE YOU WILL CREATE

6) DECISION CREATES FUTURE & FULFILLS DESTINIES.

7) DECISION BEAUTIFLIES OUR FUTURE.

8) DECISION KEEPS YOU OUT OF TROUBLE

9) DECISION EXEMPTS YOU FROM EVIL

10) DECISION GURANTEES ETERNITY

11) YOU CAN ONLY GO FAR IN LIFE BY YOUR FAITH DECISIONS.

12) YOU ARE POOR BECAUSE YOU MADE SUCH DECISIONS

13) MAKE A DECISION & CHANGE YOUR LIFE.

14) LIFE CHANGING DECISIONS IS A FUNCTION OF QUALITY INFORMATION

15) SUCCESS IN LIFE IS A FUNCTION OF DECISION.

16) LIFE EXPERIENCES IS FULL OF DECISIONS.

17) DECISIONS CHANGES DESTINIES.

18) NEVER SETTLE FOR INFORMATION ONLY LOOK FOR REVELATION

19) YOU ARE WHERE YOU ARE TODAY BASED ON YOUR LAST DECISION.

20) INFORMATION IS CRUCIAL IN DECISION MAKING

21) DECISION MAKERS RULE THE WORLD.

22) YOU CAN RULE YOUR WORLD BY QUALITY DECISIONS

23) AS LONG AS YOU DECIDE RIGHTLY SATAN CANNOT HARRASS YOU.

CHAPTER 2
OPERATING IN FREEDOM

"Therefore if any man be in Christ, he is a new creature: old things are passed away; behold, all things are become new." **2 Cor5:17**

We must be in Christ if we must operate in freedom. The scripture above says, *"… if any man be in Christ, he is a new creature: old things are passed away; behold, all things are become new."* **2 Cor5:17.**

For us to operate in freedom we must first Repent of our sins and come to the knowledge of the truth of God's word. Salvation which also means deliverance of our soul from sin and from the destruction of the devil.

HOW DO I OPERATE IN FREEDOM ONE MAY ASK?

For us to experience the free flow of favor and freedom in Christ Jesus we must engage diligently in doing the following:

Chapter 2 - Operating in Freedom

CARRY THE RIGHT MINDSET

It takes the right mindset to do the right thing at any time in our life. It is written *"And herein do I exercise myself, to have always a conscience void to offence toward God, and toward men."* **Acts24:16.**

The right mindset will exempt us from trial and tribulation. Remember.. *"And Paul, earnestly beholding the council, said, Men and brethren, I have lived in all good conscience before God until this day."* **Acts 23:1**

It is the right mindset that will deliver us from trial and tribulation in life. It will exempt us from the terrors and horrors of life. We must live our lives as free people.

Our mindset must be geared towards freedom for us to experience the same freedom. Every time we possess the right mindset we are exempted from troubles and accusations.

"Unto the pure all things are pure: but unto them that are defiled and unbelieving is nothing pure; but even their mind and conscience is defiled."
Titus1:15

RIGHTEOUSNESS AS A WAY OF LIFE

Unless we become righteous people by the way we live and conduct our lives, we will forever remain subject to false accusation, trials and tribulations. Righteousness as a way of life is a relevant key to operate in freedom in Christ Jesus.

FLEE FROM SIN AND IMMORALITIES

Every form of sin traps us in bondage. It is written *"For sin shall not have dominion over you: for ye are not under the law, but under grace."* **Romans6:14.**

Any form of sin puts us in to bondage. We are admonished by the holy bible to, flee these things; and follow after righteousness, godliness, faith, love, patience, meekness.

"Know ye not, that to whom ye yield yourselves servants to obey, his servants ye are to whom ye obey; whether of sin unto death, or of obedience unto righteousness?" **Romans 6:16**

WE MUST DEVELOP THE EVER PRESENCE OF THE JOY OF THE LORD

Although the bible says that the joy of the Lord is our strength, really the joy of the Lord attracts His presence and in His presence is fulness of joy; at thy right hand there are pleasures for evermore. This we mean His presence brings comforts and consolation hope and confidence.

FLEE FROM COMPLAINING AND MURMURING

In our lives what has happened, it is easy to recall it, but what would have happened we truly do not know. We are admonished not to complain or dispute about anything concerning our lives.

It is written *"Do all things without murmurings and disputing's"* **phil2:13.**

DEVELOP AN ATTITUDE OF GRATITUDE

For anyone to come out of depression, lack and want in life, we must develop an attitude of gratitude. We are admonished by the holy bible to give God thanks in all things in life.

"In everything give thanks: for this is the will of God in Christ Jesus concerning you." **1theo5:18**

Chapter 2 - Operating in Freedom

How do we enjoy his freedom in life?

~We must be born again and receive the free gift of salvation

What we mean by being born again means we must repent of all unrighteousness, of all sins and confess the Lord Jesus as Lord.

"For by grace are ye saved through faith; and that not of yourselves: it is the gift of God:" **Ephesians2:8**

~We must live a righteous life no matter the prevailing circumstances

Righteousness exonerates us from condemnation. The bible says *"he that doeth righteousness is righteous, even as he is righteous."* **1John3:7.**

No man/woman can operate in freedom without embracing righteousness as a lifestyle. We must repent of our sins and start doing the right thing everywhere and at any time we get the privilege to do so.

~We must not defile our life and destiny with the sin of immoralities

Immoralities defiles and dents the dignity of Christianity in life. For us to operate in freedom, we must flee from all appearance of immoralities and sin. *"For sin shall not have dominion over you: for ye are not under the law, but under grace."* **Romans6:14.**

Remember... *"For all have sinned, and come short of the glory of God;"* **Romans3:23**

~We must not ruled by alcohol or other drug substances

It is written *"And be not drunk with wine, wherein is excess; but be filled with the Spirit;"* **Ephesians5:18.**

"Some fellows have allowed alcohol to become their source of freedom from stress, trials, and challenges of life. Not given to wine, no striker, not greedy of filthy lucre; but patient, not a brawler, not covetous" **1timothy3:3**

Chapter 2 - Operating in Freedom

As long as you are not free from the chains of alcohol, you will never experience nor operate in freedom in Christ Jesus.

Remember.. *"Wine is a mocker, strong drink is raging: and whosoever is deceived thereby is not wise."* **Proverb20:1**

~We must be a husband/wife of one wife/husband if you are married

As long as anyone is jumping from one man/woman to the next they will never operate in freedom in Christ.

It is written, *"must be blameless, the husband of one wife, vigilant, sober, of good behavior, given to hospitality, apt to teach; 1timothy3:2. For us all to operate in freedom we must flee from sexual immoralities. It corrupts any man/woman. It defies any man/woman. For this is the will of God, even your sanctification, that ye should abstain from fornication."*
1theo4:3

In conclusion; freedom in Christ Jesus is free of charge but the price tag is "Sanctification" for anyone to experience it.

CONDITION TO EXPERIENCE FREEDOM IN CHRIST JESUS

REPENTANCE

The first step into freedom is repentance. When King David repented he made this outstanding statements *"Create in me a clean heart, O God; and renew a right spirit within me. Cast me not away from thy presence; and take not thy holy spirit from me. Restore unto me the joy of thy salvation; and uphold me with thy free spirit."* **Psalms 51:10-12**

We must repent to experience His freedom.

Every time we repent of our sins, God expect us to surrender also. It is the act of surrender that indicates our desire for his "Power & Freedom".

God is always willing to restore our lives as long as we are willing to repent of our sins. God said *"......for I will forgive their iniquity, and I will remember their sin no more."* **Jer31:34**

BE BAPTIZED

Our salvation is questionable without baptism. We must be baptize for our Christian walk (Christ like) walk to be complete and secured.

".... be baptized every one of you in the name of Jesus Christ for the remission of sins, and ye shall receive the gift of the Holy Ghost." **Acts2:38.**

"We must be baptized to operate in freedom. Now when all the people were baptized, it came to pass, that Jesus also being baptized, and praying, the heaven was opened, And the Holy Ghost descended in a bodily shape like a dove upon him, and a voice came from heaven, which said, Thou art my beloved Son; in thee I am well pleased." **Luke3:21-22.**

CONFESS OF YOUR SIN

No one is entitled to experience His "Freedom & Power" unless we confess and forsake our sins. If we confess our sins, he is faithful and just to forgive us our sins, and to cleanse us from all unrighteousness. **1John1:9**

Confession is the gateway to experience his freedom and power. Among all the plat form to enjoy total liberty is confession of our sins.

ACKNOWLEDGMENT

It is our Christian duty to acknowledge the Lord Jesus as savior.

Every time we acknowledge the Lord Jesus as Lord & Savior, God takes note, As the sovereign God he release us from every other power contrary to our redemption and frees us to experience true salvation. Acknowledge that you are a sinner and that Jesus Christ died for your sins.
Rom3:23.

Chapter 2 - Operating in Freedom

BORN AGAIN

As simple as it sound we must be born again if we must operate in freedom the remaining days of our lives. Jesus answered and said unto him, Verily, verily, I say unto thee, Except a man be born again, he cannot see the kingdom of God.

"Except a man be born of water and of the Spirit, he cannot enter into the kingdom of God. That which is born of the flesh is flesh; and that which is born of the Spirit is spirit. Marvel not that I said unto thee, Ye must be born again." **John3:3,5-7.**

SUMMARY OF CHAPTER TWO

~We must repent for God to restore and grant us freedom

~We must confess Jesus as Lord for us to operate in freedom.

~ We must practice righteousness if we must operate in freedom.

~ We must develop a positive mentality that all things are possible.

~ We must develop an optimistic mindset.

~We must believe that we will emerge victorious in life against all odd regardless of the circumstances and prevailing challenges.

CHAPTER 3
EXPERIENCING FREEDOM IN CHRIST

"Unto the pure all things are pure: but unto them that are defiled and unbelieving is nothing pure; but even their mind and conscience is defiled."
Titus 1:15

WHAT IS FREEDOM?

Freedom means the power or right to act, speak, or think as one wants without hindrance or restraint from anyone persons or spirits.

It is the absence of subjection to foreign domination or despotic government: Freedom is the state of not being imprisoned or enslaved by any person or any demonic spirit. It is the state of being physically unrestricted and able to move, worship, breakthrough in life, experience promotion in careers and bear children in marriages.

It is the state of not being subject to or affected by (a particular evil spirits).

> *"Freedom is the power of self-determination attributed to the will; the quality of being independent of fate or necessity. It is inevitable for us to proclaim Jesus as Lord with us experiencing lavish freedom in our lives. If the Son therefore shall make you free, ye shall be free indeed."*
> **John 8:36.**

Freedom consists not in doing what we like, but in having the right to do what we ought ---------**Pope John Paul 11**

For us to experience freedom in our lives we must become Gods children and servant, otherwise we are not part of His divine freedom for all His children and servants. So many folks in the church of Christ have never experience freedom in Christ because they lack the knowledge of the truth of God's word.

As long as you are proud and arrogant, as long as you are not ready to become a child and servant of God, you will never experience this dimension of freedom in life.

Chapter 3 - Experiencing Freedom in Christ

"But as many as received him, to them gave he power to become the sons of God, even to them that believe on his name:" **John1:12**.

As believer we must have an encounter with the unquestionable dimension of God's freedom. So many believers complain of night mares and dream of attack in the night because they are not free from this earthy immoral things. Freedom in Jesus Christ is not attainable without faith in God. And Jesus answering saith unto them, Have faith in God.
Mark11:22

As believers we must recognize that we are seated on high with Christ Jesus far above principalities and power.

"And hath raised us up together, and made us sit together in heavenly places in Christ Jesus:"
Ephesians2:6.

We must be pure in our heart and have no bitterness nor fear against anyone. It is written *" For ye have not received the spirit of bondage again to fear; but ye have received the Spirit of adoption, whereby we cry, Abba, Father."* **Romans 8:15**

There are a lot of us, great believers but we need deliverance and an encounter with the truth of God's word.

HOW DO I ENCOUNTER HIS FREEDOM?

We must receive Him.

"But as many as received him, to them gave he power to become the sons of God, even to them that believe on his name." **John 1:12**

We must believe in Him.

"... Believe on the Lord Jesus Christ, and thou shalt be saved, and thy house." **Acts 16:31**

We must obey Him

"If they obey and serve him, they shall spend their days in prosperity, and their years in pleasures." **Job36:11**

We must have faith in God

"And Jesus answering saith unto them, Have faith in God" **Mark11:22**

We must serve Him

"And ye shall serve the Lord your God, and he shall bless thy bread, and thy water; and I will take sickness away from the midst of thee." **Exodus23:25.**

So many of us have developed the wrong thinking. The power and presence of God is not in words. Too much talking will not bring his presence down.

"For the kingdom of God is not in word, but in power." **1cor4:20.**

It is written, *"For I am not ashamed of the gospel of Christ: for it is the power of God unto salvation to everyone that believeth; to the Jew first, and also to the Greek."*
Romans1:16

In my own understanding, as long as we follow these few outlines above, we will inevitably experience his freedom and power in our life time.

BIBLICAL CHARACTERS THAT EXPERIENCED HIS FREEDOM

Apostle Paul

Apostle Paul used run around the city of Jerusalem persecuting Christians until he encountered Jesus on his way to Damascus. Apostle Paul left a remarkable legacy for us all to follow. I pray may you encounter Gods dimension power, a new dimension of a higher order that will change your story the remaining days of your life.

Chapter 3 - Experiencing Freedom in Christ

Joseph

The life story of Joseph is a typical example for every Christian to emulate. This young man from the age of 17 was despised by his brothers, sold into Egypt, became a slave and a prisoner but God vindicated him and made him deputy to the king of Egypt Pharaoh. Joseph encountered God in his life time. I prophesy unto you may you encounter God in your life time.

Daniel

Daniel who because of Gods favor lived to see four seating presidents come and go. The hand of God was heavy upon the life of Daniel in the bible.

"Now God had brought Daniel into favour and tender love with the prince of the eunuchs." **Daniel1:9.**

DO YOU WANT TO EXPERIENCE HIS FREEDOM?

Repent and turn away from our wicked ways

If truly we all want to see his power and his glory we must learn to do well at all times. We are encouraged by the Holy bible that evil bow before the good; and the wicked at the gates of the righteous. Proverb14:19.

Believe me when I say these things. It is true. All evil men are going to hell, there are no two ways about it. As long as you practice evil, as long as you are doing what God hates, you are heading into hell. But we all have a chance to repent in life and God will restore our lives.

We must come to the knowledge of the Lord Jesus Christ

Do you know him? The bible says *" And why call ye me, Lord, Lord, and do not the things which I say?"* **Luke6:46.**

We must get to know him if we desire an encounter with his presence, freedom and power in our lives. Jesus said *"But I know him: for I am from him, and he hath sent me."* **John7:29**

HINDRACE TO FREEDOM IN CHRIST

WICKEDNESS IN LIFE

The Holy Spirit will never grant anyone an encounter as long as they operate in wickedness. But them that are without God judgeth. Therefore put away from among yourselves that wicked person. **1cor5:13.**

Do you remember the man Saul? The first king of Isreal, despite his reign God did not know him at the end because of his wicked ness in his life time. *"..... the shield of Saul, as though he had not been anointed with oil."* **2samuel1:21**

We all fall from grace every time we engage in wickedness and bitterness of the heart as a lifestyle.

"Looking diligently lest any man fail of the grace of God; lest any root of bitterness springing up trouble you, and thereby many be defiled;" **Hebrew12:15.**

Wickedness as a lifestyle will hinder anyone from experiencing his power, presence, and freedom in life.

LIVING IN SIN

Every time we live in sin we end up in a defeated lifestyle. But whenever you live in righteousness, we live a victorious life. Sin bring judgement against us. Sin is the gateway for the perpetrator to accuse and torment us in life. I pray, sin shall not have dominion over our lives in the mighty Name of Jesus.

"Behold, the Lord's hand is not shortened, that it cannot save; neither his ear heavy that it cannot hear: But your iniquities have separated between you and your God, and your sins have hid his face from you, that he will not hear."
Isaiah59:1-2.

The presence of sin in our lives will hinder anyone from experiencing his power, presence, and freedom in life. We are admonished by the Holy bible

" Turn you at my reproof: behold, I will pour out my spirit unto you, I will make known my words unto you." **Porverb1:23**

LIVING WITH UNFORGIVING SPIRIT

"As long as you do not forgive others, our heavenly father will not forgive us. For if ye forgive men their trespasses, your heavenly Father will also forgive you: But if ye forgive not men their trespasses, neither will your Father forgive your trespasses." **Mathew6:14-15.**

The above scripture simplified what I meant by living in un-forgiveness in life.

REGRET

As long as we keep looking backward in life by regretting and pondering what would have happened or if I did it this way or that way, we will never move forward.

"And Jesus said unto him, No man, having put his hand to the plough, and looking back, is fit for the kingdom of God." **Luke 9:62.**

Learn to appreciate how far God has brought you and move forward hence forth. One man said and I quote *"when you are depressed, you are living in the past, when you are anxious you are living in the future, but when you are at peace you are living in the present."*

It is written *"Remember ye not the former things, neither consider the things of old. Behold, I will do a new thing; now it shall spring forth; shall ye not know it? I will even make a way in the wilderness, and rivers in the desert."*
Isaiah 43:18-19

Chapter 3 - Experiencing Freedom in Christ

ACCESS TO THE HOLY SPIRIT

BE BORN AGAIN

"Salvation begins with new birth. Until you are born again, you do not know Him. But as many as received him, to them gave he power to become the sons of God, even to them that believe on his name." **John1:12**.

Until you are born again you do not have access to the Holy Spirit.

THE FEAR OF GOD

"Unless you embrace the virtue and characteristics to fear, respect and honor God, you will never have access to the Holy Spirit. The fear of the Lord is the beginning of wisdom: and the knowledge of the holy is understanding." **Proverb 9:10**

RIGHTEOUS LIFESTYLE

Righteousness is a lifestyle that must be engrafted by all believers, if we must have unlimited access into his presence.

> *"And the work of righteousness shall be peace; and the effect of righteousness quietness and assurance forever."*
> **Isaiah 32:17**

Righteousness is the access key to provoke the person & presence of the Holy Spirit.

INTEGRITY

God will judge all our lives. Until you clean up and embrace integrity as a lifestyle you will never have access to the Holy spirit.

> *"The integrity of the upright shall guide them:……."*
> **Proverb 11:3**

AGREEMENT

Unless we agree with the Holy Spirit, we are not permitted to have access into His presence.

> *"Can two walk together, except they be agreed?"*
> **Amos 3:3**

THE RIGHT WORDS

There is great power in the words that we speak daily to ourselves and to our oppositions and challenges in life. ***Job 6:25*** declares How forcible are right words! Jesus said there is no idle word in the kingdom.

Speaking the right word anytime will grant us unlimited access into His presence in life.

"Suffer not thy mouth to cause thy flesh to sin; neither say thou before the angel, that it was an error: wherefore should God be angry at thy voice, and destroy the work of thine hands?"
Eccl5:6

SOUL WINNING

Unless we win souls for the Father we are not qualified to enter to his presence and enjoy unlimited access with the Holy Spirit.

> *"Go ye therefore, and teach all nations, baptizing them in the name of the Father, and of the Son, and of the Holy Ghost: Teaching them to observe all things whatsoever I have commanded you: and, lo, I am with you always, even unto the end of the world."*
> **Mathew28:19-20**

OBEDIENCE

Obey the Holy Spirit and you shall enjoy his unlimited access in your life.

> *"But if thou shalt indeed obey his voice, and do all that I speak; then I will be an enemy unto thine enemies, and an adversary unto thine adversaries."*
> **Exodus23:22**

PRAY IN THE SPIRIT

Every time we pray in the spirit you are not speaking to men but unto GOD. Every time we pray in the spirit we provoke access into his presence.

Chapter 3 - Experiencing Freedom in Christ

"For he that speaketh in an unknown tongue speaketh not unto men, but unto God: for no man understandeth him; howbeit in the spirit he speaketh mysteries."
1cor 14:2

SUMMARY OF CHAPTER 3

~ It takes the presence and power of God for anyone to experience his freedom.

~ Freedom in God is free of charge but we must be diligently involved.

~As long as you receive him , he will grant you power to become His son.

~There is always a thing for us to do to provoke his power, presence freedom, and liberty. We must all go into a deep search of what to do.

~ Repentance is the gateway into restoration power and freedom in our lives.

~You will secure His presence if you do what provokes his power.

~ As long as you do well, you will make heaven at last.

SUMMARY

"Now the Lord is that Spirit: and where the Spirit of the Lord is, there is liberty." **2 cor3:17**

The truth of what we have been saying all along in this book is that He- JESUS, died for our freedom and liberty. But because he lives, we shall live also. God want us all to live in freedom.

It is written *"For God hath not given us the spirit of fear; but of power, and of love, and of a sound mind."* **2timothy1:8.**

We must allow this mentality to keep glowing everyday of our lives if we must live in victory freedom and power in life.

Chapter 3 - Experiencing Freedom in Christ

Remember………..

"For ye have not received the spirit of bondage again to fear; but ye have received the Spirit of adoption, whereby we cry, Abba, Father." **Romans8:15.**

With reference to the subject matter, freedom in life is a mentality. The bible called it overcomer's mentality.

"For whatsoever is born of God overcometh the world: and this is the victory that overcometh the world, even our faith." **1John5:4.**

It is the ability to stay positive, remain optimistic against all contradiction. It is a mind set to expect the best out of the worst scenario. We must develop this mindset, nurture and enforce it in our lives as we grow and encounter obstacles and other hindering challenges of life.

"Him that overcometh will I make a pillar in the temple of my God, and he shall go no more out..." **Rev3:12.**

May I say this to you in closing? Repent of your sins and ask God for an encounter in your prayer. May you encounter his freedom the remaining days of your life in the Mighty Name of Jesus. **Amen**

"Let us hear the conclusion of the whole matter: Fear God, and keep his commandments: for this is the whole duty of man.

For God shall bring every work into judgment, with every secret thing, whether it be good, or whether it be evil." **Eccl12:13-14**

Whatever that I have been saying all along in this book, remains a story unless God grant you an encounter of the mystery of freedom. Remember, you cannot get an encounter if you do not know him.

Chapter 3 - Experiencing Freedom in Christ

The bible says in Eccl: 12:14 For God shall bring every work into judgment, with every secret thing, whether it be good, or whether it be evil.

If you are a born again Christian; we like to encourage you in your Christian life. If you are not a born again Christian we can help you here receive genuine salvation.

Therefore if any man be in Christ, he is a new creature: old things are passed away; behold, all things are become new.

Now repeat this Prayer after me.

Say Lord Jesus, I accept you today, as my Lord and my savior, forgive me of my sins wash me with your blood. Right now, I believe, I am sanctified, I am save, I am free, I am free from the Power of sin to serve the Lord Jesus. Thank you Lord for saving me. **Amen.**

Congratulations:

YOU ARE NOW A BORN AGAIN CHRISTIAN

CONGRATULATIONS!!

What must I do to determine my divine visitation?

To determine divine visitation you must be born again

The word says as many as received him, to them gave He power to become the sons of God. Even to them that believe on his name.

To qualify for divine visitation do the following sincerely,

1) Acknowledge that you are a sinner and that He died for you. **Rom3:23.**

2) Repent of your sins. **Acts 3:19, Luke13:5, 2Peter3:9**

Chapter 3 - Experiencing Freedom in Christ

3) Believe in your heart that Jesus died for your sin. **Romans10:10**

4) Confess Jesus as the Lord over your life. **Romans10:10, Acts2:21**

Now repeat this Prayer after me

Say Lord Jesus, I accept you today, as my Lord and my savior, forgive me of my sins wash me with your blood. Right now, I believe, I am sanctified, I am save, I am free, I am free from the Power of sin to serve the Lord Jesus. Thank you Lord for saving me. Amen.

Congratulations:

YOU ARE NOW A BORN AGAIN CHRISTIAN

AGAIN I SAY TO YOU CONGRATULATIONS

I adjure you to watch the Spirit of God bear witness with your Spirit confirming His word with signs following. The word says The Spirit itself beareth witness with our spirit, that we are the children of God.

Join a bible believing church or join us on our weekly and Sunday worship services at 343 Sanford Avenue Newark New Jersey 07106.

WISDOM KEYS

Every Productive Society is a society heading to the top

Millions of Nigerians run away from Nigeria, very few Nigerians stay in Nigeria.

My decision to return Nigeria is the will of God for my life

My short coming in America after 18 years, trained me to be wise, to think, reflect and reason appropriately.

Chapter 3 - Experiencing Freedom in Christ

If you train your mind to reason it will train your hands to earn money.

It is absurd to use the money of the heathen to build the kingdom of the living God.

Every Ministry reveals its agenda and goal either at the beginning or at the end. Be careful of your life it is your first Ministry.

The average American mind is conditioned for a continual quest to get new things and (discard the former) and throw away old things.

When I considered well, my BMW jeep became my initial deposit for the work of the ministry in Nigeria

Everyone is waiting for you to change your mind until you change your thinking nothing changes around you.

Multiple academic degrees in other discipline gave me the chance to think, reflect and reason

What so everyone are thinking and reflecting at the moment reveals you to the time and the now factor

All events and intents are the product of precise thought processes, accurate reason every event is designed for a designated timeline

Wisdom is your ability to think, to create and invent. If you can think wise enough you will come out of penury

The distance between you and success is your creative ability to think reason and reflect accurate.

Success is the result of hard work, commitment resolve and determination learning from past mistakes and failing.

If you organize your mind you have organized your life and destiny.

Chapter 3 - Experiencing Freedom in Christ

There is a thin line between success and failure. If you look above and beyond you are on your way to success.

Wealth is your ability to think, power is your ability to reason and success is your ability to be informed.

If you can make use of your mind by thinking and reasoning God will make use of your life and destiny.

Think and Be Great

Reflect, Reason, think and be great

Famous people are born of woman

That you will make it is your intention; that you will survive is your resolve, that you will succeed with changes is your determination, personal efforts and hard work.

No man was born a failure. Lack of vision is the end product of failure.

Working with mental patients encourages and aspire me to be a productive observant and dedicated to my assignment.

Successful people are not magicians, it is the will power combined with hard work, and determination and a resolve to succeed that make them succeed.

In the unequivocal state of the mind, intention is not a location or a position it is the state of the mind.

So many people think that they think. The mind is used to think reflect and reason. You will remain blind with your eye open until you can see with your mind by thinking.

There is no favoritism in accurate and precise calculation

Although knowledge is power, information is the key and gateway to a great future.

It will take the hand of God to move the hand of man.

Chapter 3 - Experiencing Freedom in Christ

With the backing of the great wise God, nothing will disconnect you from your inheritance.

As long as you have wisdom and understanding of God, Satan and evil cannot manipulate your life and destiny.

You have come this far by yourself judgment and decision you have made in the past, now lean and listen to God for another dimension of greatness.

Great people are common people it is extra ordinary effort and the price of sacrifice that produces greatness.

As a mental direct care worker I saw a great pastor and a motivational speaker within myself.

Menial job does not reduce your self-worth, until you resolve to achieve greatness see greatness in all you do; you will never count in your community

The principle of Jesus will solve your gambling and addiction problems

The man of Jesus will lead you into heaven,

Everyone have their self-appraisal and what they think about you. Until you discover yourself other opinion about you will alter the real you.

Supervisors and directors are just a position in the chain of command in a work place. Never allow your supervisor hierarchy to alter your opinion about yourself.

Everyone can come out of debt if they make up their mind.

That I am not a decision maker at work does not diminish my contribution to my world.

Although it appears like it was a poor decision to accept a direct care employment at a psychiatric hospital as I reflect of my nine years of experience, it became apparent that I have learnt and experienced enough for my next assignment.

Chapter 3 - Experiencing Freedom in Christ

Self-encouragement and determination is a resolve of the heart.

If you are determined to make a difference, and do the things that make a difference you will eventually make a difference.

Good things do not come easy

Short cuts will cut your life short.

Those who look ahead move ahead.

Life is all about making an impact. In your life time strive to make an impact in your community.

Make friends and connect with people who are moving ahead of you in life.

If you can look around well you have come a long way in your life, made a lot of difference and realized a lot of success in life.

If you are my old friend, hurry up to reach out to me before I become a stranger to you.

The Price of Freedom by Franklin N. Abazie

Everything I am blessed with inspirations from God, that change my definition and interpretation of the world around me.

I thought I was stagnant and lonely until I looked around and noticed my children running around and my wife cooking.

At 40 I resigned my Job to seek the Lord forever.

My ministry took a drastic rise to the top when the wisdom of God visited me with knowledge and understanding.

You will be a better person if you understand the characteristics of your personality – your mood swings attitudes and habits.

It is the seed of love you sow into the heart of a child and a woman that you reap in due time.

Love is not selfish, love share everything including the concealed secrets of the mind.

As long as you have a prayer life and a bible; you will never feel lonely, rejected and idle in the race of life.

Chapter 3 - Experiencing Freedom in Christ

When good friends disconnect from you, let them go, they might have seen something new in a different direction.

Confidence in yourself and in God is the only way to bring you out of captivity

Never train a child to waste his/her time.

The mind is the greatest assets of a great future.

You walk by common sense run by principles and fly by instruction.

Those who fly in flight of life fly alone.

Up in the air you are alone. No one can toll you accept the compass of knowledge and information

I have seen a tolling vehicle I have seen a tolling ship I have never seen a tolling airplane.

I exercise my judgment and make a decision every minute of the day.

Decisions are crucial, critical and vital with reference to your future.

So many people wish for a great future. You can only work towards a great future.

Your celebrity status began when you discovered your talent. What are you good at? Work at it with all commitment.

Prayers will sustain you but the wisdom of God will prosper you.

When I met Oyedepo, his teachings changed my perspective, but when I met Ibiyeomie; His teaching changed my perception.

I will be successful in ministry if only I concentrate and focus my energy in the work of the ministry.

It took the late Dr. Vincent Pearle Norman's book to open my mind towards kingdom success.

FAVOR CONFESSION

Father thank you for making me righteous and accepted through the blood of Jesus Christ. Because of that, I am blessed and highly favored by God. I am the subject of your affection. Your favor surrounds me as a shield, and the first thing that people see around me is your favored shield.

Thank you that I have favor with you and man today. All day long people go out of their way to bless me and help me. I have favor with everyone that I deal with today. Doors that were once closed are now opened for me. I receive preferential treatment, and I have special privileges, I am Gods favored child.

No good thing will he withhold from me. Because of Gods favor my enemies cannot triumph over my life. I have supernatural increase and promotion.

I declare restoration to everything that the devil has stolen from my life. I have honor in the midst of my adversaries and an increase in assets, especially in real estate and expansion of territories.

Because I am highly favored by God, I experience great victories, supernatural turnarounds, and miraculous breakthrough in the midst of great impossibilities. I receive recognition, prominence, and honor. Petitions are granted to me even by ungodly authorities. Policies, rules, regulations, and laws are changed and reverse on my behalf.

I win battles that I don't even have to fight, because God fights them for me. This is the day, the set time and the designated moment for me to experience the free favor of God, that profusely and lavishly abound on my behalf in Jesus name.

Amen.

Chapter 3 - Experiencing Freedom in Christ

YOU MUST BE BORN AGAIN

If you are a born again Christian; we like to encourage you in your Christian life. If you are not a born again Christian we can help you here receive genuine salvation.

"Therefore if any man be in Christ, he is a new creature: old things are passed away; behold, all things are become new." **2cor5:17**

Now repeat this Prayer after me

Say Lord Jesus, I accept you today, as my Lord and my savior, forgive me of my sins wash me with your blood. Right now, I believe, I am sanctified, I am save, I am free, I am free from the Power of sin to serve the Lord Jesus. Thank you Lord for saving me. **Amen.**

Congratulations:

YOU ARE NOW A BORN AGAIN CHRISTIAN

AGAIN I SAY TO YOU CONGRATULATIONS

What must I do to determine my divine visitation?

To determine divine visitation you must be born again! The word says as many as received him, to them gave He power to become the sons of God. Even to them that believe on his name

To qualify for divine visitation do the following sincerely,

1) Acknowledge that you are a sinner and that He died for you. **Rom3:23.**

2) Repent of your sins. **Acts 3:19, Luke13:5, 2Peter3:9**

3) Believe in your heart that Jesus died for your sin. **Romans10:10**

4) Confess Jesus as the Lord over your life. **Romans10:10, Acts2:21**

Say Lord Jesus, I accept you today, as my Lord and my savior, forgive me of my sins wash me with your blood. Right now, I believe, I am sanctified, I am save, I am free, I am free from the Power of sin to serve the Lord Jesus. Thank you Lord for saving me. Amen.

Congratulations:

YOU ARE NOW A BORN AGAIN CHRISTIAN

AGAIN I SAY TO YOU CONGRATULATIONS

I adjure you to watch the Spirit of God bear witness with your Spirit confirming His word with signs following. The word says The Spirit itself beareth witness with our spirit, that we are the children of God.

Join a bible believing church or join us on our weekly and Sunday worship services at 343 Sanford Avenue Newark New Jersey 07106.

CHAPTER 4
PRAYER OF SALVATION

I am glad you have read this book all the way from the beginning to this point. All I have said from the beginning will remain a mystery until you commit it into practice.

And before you do so I want you, if you have not given your life to Jesus to do so now. Give your life to Christ. I want you to know the truth! The truth is that Jesus died for your sins and because He died you must be alive and prosperous.

What must I do to determine my divine visitation?

To determine divine visitation you must be born again! The word says as many as received him, to them gave He power to become the sons of God. Even to them that believe on his name

To qualify for divine visitation do the following sincerely,

Chapter 4 - Prayer of Salvation

1) Acknowledge that you are a sinner and that He died for you.Rom3:23.

2) Repent of your sins. Acts 3:19, Luke13:5, 2Peter3:9

3) Believe in your heart that Jesus died for your sin.Romans10:10

4) Confess Jesus as the Lord over your life. Romans10:10, Acts2:21

Now repeat this Prayer after me

Say Lord Jesus, I accept you today, as my Lord and my savior, forgive me of my sins wash me with your blood. Right now, I believe, I am sanctified, I am save, I am free, I am free from the Power of sin to serve the Lord Jesus. Thank you Lord for saving me. **Amen.**

Congratulations:

YOU ARE NOW A BORN AGAIN CHRISTIAN

AGAIN I SAY TO YOU CONGRATULATIONS

I adjure you to watch the Spirit of God bear witness with your Spirit confirming His word with signs following. The word says The Spirit itself beareth witness with our spirit, that we are the children of God.

MIRACLE CARE OUTREACH

"...But that the members should have the same care one for another" **1cor12:25**

We are all members of the body of Christ. Jesus commanded us to love our neighbor as ourselves. This includes caring for one another as a member of one body. True love is expressed in caring and giving. The word says for God so Love He gave....

Reach out to someone in need of Jesus, help someone in crisis find Christ. Look out and prove your love to Jesus by caring and inviting your friends and associates to find Jesus the Healer.

Invite your friends to our Home Care Cell Fellowship (Miracle chapel Intl Satellite fellowship) In the USA at 33 Schley Street Newark New Jersey 07112.

If you are in Nigeria—MIRACLE OF GOD MINISTRIES

A.K.A "MIRACLE CHAPEL INTL" Mpama –Egbu-Owerri Imo state Nigeria.

(Home Care Cell fellowship Group). We meet every Tuesday at 6:00pm-7:00pm.

LIFE IS NOT ALL ABOUT DURATION BUT ITS ALL ABOUT DONATION

What does the above statement mean?....

"Life consists not in accumulation of material wealth." **Luke 12:15.**

But it's all about liberality….meaning- *"what you can give and share with others."* **Proverb 11:25.**

When you live for others--You live forever- because you out live your generation by the legacy you live behind after you depart into glory to be with the Lord.

But when you live to yourself - you are reduced to self—you are easily forgotten when you die and depart in glory.

Permit me to admonish you today to live your life to be a blessing to a soul connected to you today. I want you to know that so many souls are connected and looking up to you, and through you so many souls will be saved and rescued from destruction. Will you disciple someone today to find Jesus Christ?

Chapter 4 - Prayer of Salvation

"As a genuine Christian; it is your duty to evangelize Jesus Christ to all you meet on your way. Jesus is still in the healing business-Jesus is still doing miracles from time of old to now. Therefore tell someone about Jesus Christ today, disciple and bring them to Church."
John 1:45 Philip findeth Nathanael….

Please to prove the sincerity of your love for God today; please become a soul winner. The dignity of your Christianity is hidden in your boldness to proclaim and evangelize Jesus Christ to all you meet on your way. There is a question mark on the integrity of your Christianity until you become a life soul winner. Invite someone to join us worship the Lord Jesus this coming Sunday. Amen

MIRACLE OF GOD MINISTRIES
PILLARS OF THE COMMISSION

We Believe Preach and Practice the following,

1) We believe and preach Salvation to every living human being

2) We believe and preach Repentance and forgiveness of sins

3) We believe and preach the baptism of the Holy Spirit and Spiritual gifts

4) We believe and teach the Prosperity

5) We believe and preach Divine Healing and Miracles (Signs & Wonder)

6) We believe and preach Faith

7) We believe and Proclaim the Power of God (Supernatural)

8) We believe and Proclaim Praise & Worship to God

9) We believe and preach Wisdom

10) We believe and preach Holiness (Consecration)

11) We believe and preach Vision

12) We believe and teach the Word of God

13) We believe and teach Success

14) We believe and practice Prayer

15) We believe and teach Deliverance

This 15 stones form the Pillars of Our Commission.

Become part of this church family and follow this great move of God

MY HEART FELT PRAYER FOR YOU

One of our primary objective as a ministry is to simplify the truth of God word to everyone's understanding. As a servant of God, I desire to see you encounter Jesus Christ for yourself. It will please the master today if you will repent of any known or known sin in your life.

I desire to see you saved and engrafted into the house of God. Most of my works are directed to reach people like you. We are always willing to explain the truth of the birth, ministry, death, and coming of the Lord Jesus Christ.

A few of my other books will also strike some heavenly revelation to your spirit. Please get hold of any of our teachings, either in DVD, s MP3, sermons, teaching, books, materials and tapes.

It will richly be of a blessing to you. I guarantee you this!!

Now let me Pray for you

Sovereign God of freedom, I come to you today boldly seeking you presence and power to make a difference in the life of this precious one reading this nugget. I pray Father of mercy to grant us the audience to witness your power and freedom in every area of our lives in the Mighty Name of Jesus.

May this precious one reading this book encounter your manifold wisdom, in its uncomplicated and infinite variety. Lord prove yourself mighty with a testimony. May all who get the privilege to read this book come to the knowledge of your truth. Prove to all around my world that you sent me to impacting healing & miracles to my generation. I thank you Jesus for hearing me. Amen

ETERNITY IS REAL

It will profit us nothing as a ministry if you finish reading this book without making plans for heaven. You must make conscious plans to make heaven because eternity is real. Indeed we live in an immoral time, sin has gained grounds and promotion that even the righteous are tempted to fall short of the glory of God.

You might ask me, what must I do to be saved?

As long as we believe and repent God is willing to forgive and to restore our lives *"And they said, Believe on the Lord Jesus Christ, and thou shalt be saved, and thy house."* **Acts16:31**.

"Salvation is possible only through the name of our Lord Jesus Christ. Neither is there salvation in any other: for there is none other name under heaven given among men, whereby we must be saved." **Acts4:12.**

I admonish you therefore to think twice before you commit those sins that not only easily beset you but also separates you far away from God. As long as you repent even now, God is more than willing to restore and save your life from eternal hell fire.

"And make straight paths for your feet, lest that which is lame be turned out of the way; but let it rather be healed. Follow peace with all men, and holiness, without which no man shall see the Lord"

Hebrew12:13-14.

Make conscious plans to make heaven. Change the way you approach things and God will restore and forgive you of all your sins. Amen

ENCOUNTER WITH HIS PRESENCE

Moses cried for His presence

"Now therefore, I pray thee, if I have found grace in thy sight, shew me now thy way, that I may know thee, that I may find grace in thy sight: and consider that this nation is thy people. And he said, My presence shall go with thee, and I will give thee rest. And he said unto him, if thy presence go not with me, carry us not up hence." **Exodus33:13-15**

It takes his presence to defeat all opposition to our breakthrough and promotion in life. I pray you encounter his presence in the mighty Name of Jesus.

ENCOUNTER WITH HIS POWER

David lamented for His Power

"God, thou art my God; early will I seek thee: my soul thirsteth for thee, my flesh longeth for thee in a dry and thirsty land, where no water is; To see thy power and thy glory, so as I have seen thee in the sanctuary."

Pslams63:1-2

David took advantage of the power dimension of God to wage warfare and defeat all those who picked up a battle against him. I pray you encounter his power that makes a difference in your life time in the mighty name of Jesus.

CHAPTER 4
ABOUT THE AUTHOR

Rev Franklin N Abazie is the founding and Presiding Pastor of Miracle of God Ministries with headquarters in Newark, New Jersey USA and a branch church in Owerri- Imo State Nigeria. He is following the footsteps of one of his mentors, Oral Roberts (Healing Evangelist) of the blessed memory.

The Lord passed Oral Roberts healing mantle two days before he went to be with the Lord at age 91 into the hand of healing evangelist-Rev Franklin N Abazie in a vision.

In all his services the Power and Presence of God is present to heal all in his audience. He is an ordained man of God with a Healing Ministry reviving the healing and miracle ministry of Jesus Christ of Nazareth.

Pastor Franklin N Abazie, is called by God with a unique mandate:

"THE MOMENT IS DUE TO IMPACT YOUR WORLD THROUGH THE REVIVAL OF THE HEALING & MIRACLE MINISTRY OF JESUS CHRIST OF NAZARETH
I AM SENDING YOU TO RESTORE HEALTH UNTO THEE AND I WILL HEAL THEE OF THY WOUNDS. SAID THE LORD OF HOST"

He is a gifted ardent Teacher of the word of God who operates also in the office of a Prophet, generating and attracting undeniable signs & wonders, special miracles and healings, with apostolic fireworks of the Holy Ghost.

He is the founding and presiding senior Pastor of this fast growing Healing ministry.

Chapter 5 - About the Author

He has written over 86 inspirational, healing and transforming books covering almost all aspect of divine healing and life. He is happily married and blessed with children.

BOOKS BY REV FRANKLIN N ABAZIE

1) Commanding Abundance
2) The outcome of faith
3) Understanding the secret of prevailing prayers
4) Understanding the secret of the man God uses
5) Activating my due Season
6) Overcoming Divine Verdicts
7) The Outcome of Divine Wisdom
8) Understanding God's Restoration Mandate
9) Walking in the Victory and Authority of the truth
10) Gods Covenant Exemption
11) Destiny Restoration Pillars
12) Provoking Acceptable Praise
13) Understanding Divine Judgment
14) Activating Angelic Re-enforcement
15) Provoking Un-Merited Favor
16) The Benefits of the Speaking faith
17) Understanding Divine Arrangement

18) Understanding Divine Healing
19) The Mystery of Endurance
20) Obeying Divine Instructions
21) Understanding the Voice of God
22) Never give up on Hope
23) The prevailing Power of faith
24) Understanding Divine Prosperity
25) The Reward of Prayer
26) Covenant Keys to Answered Prayers
27) Activating the Forces of Vengeance
28) Put your faith to work
29) Where is your trust?
30) The Audacity of the Blood of Jesus
31) Redeeming Your Days
32) The force of Vision
33) Breaking the shackles of Family Curses
34) Wisdom for Marriage Stability
35) The winners Faith
36) The Prayer solution
37) The power of Prayer
38) Prayer strategy
39) The prayer that works
40) Walking in Forgiveness
41) The power of the grace of God

42) The power of Persistence
43) Overcoming Divine verdicts
44) The audacity of the blood of Jesus.
45) The prevailing power of the blood of Jesus
46) The benefit of the speaking faith.
47) Fearless faith
48) Redeeming Your Days.
49) The Supernatural Power of Prophecy
50) The companionship of the Holy Spirit
51) Understanding Divine Judgement
52) Understanding Divine Prosperity
53) Dominating Controlling Forces
54) The winners Faith
55) Destiny Restoration Pillars
56) Developing Spiritual Muscles
57) Inexplicable faith
58) The lifestyle of Prayer
59) Developing a positive attitude in life.
60) The mystery of Divine supply
61) Encounter with God's Power
62) Walking in love
63) Praying in the Spirit
64) How to provoke your testimony

65) Walking in the reality of the Anointing
66) The reality of new birth
67) The price of freedom
68) The Supernatural power of faith
69) The Power of Persistence
70) The intellectual components of Redemption
71) Overcoming Fear
72) The Force of Vision
73) Overcoming Prevailing Challenges
74) The Power of the Grace of God
75) My life & Ministry
76) The Mystery of Praise

MIRACLE OF GOD MINISTRIES

NIGERIA CRUSADE 2012

MIRACLE OF GOD MINISTRIES

NIGERIA CRUSADE

2012

MIRACLE OF GOD MINISTRIES

NIGERIA CRUSADE

2012

www.ingramcontent.com/pod-product-compliance
Lightning Source LLC
Chambersburg PA
CBHW021155080526
44588CB00008B/352